MW01135506

NAME: _____

SCHOOL: _____

PROGRAM NAME: _____

YEAR: _____

This book has been formatted small to be used on the field by students during the learning phase of their show. It has been sized to fit in a back pocket and not fall out. If the student needs to, they can punch two holes through the book just to the right of the spine, run a string through both holes and tie the ends of the strings together so the book can be worn around their neck.

Set #   Counts   Notes:

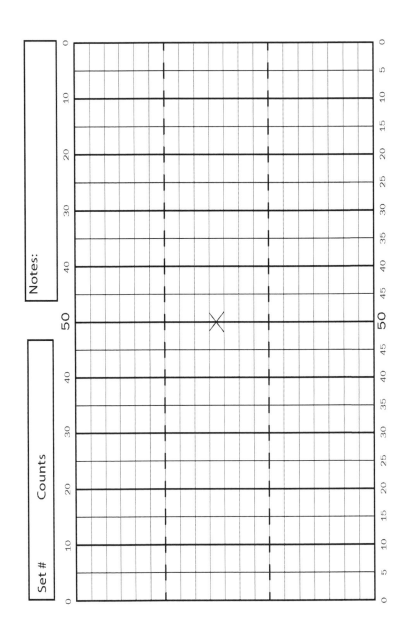

Set #   Counts   Notes:

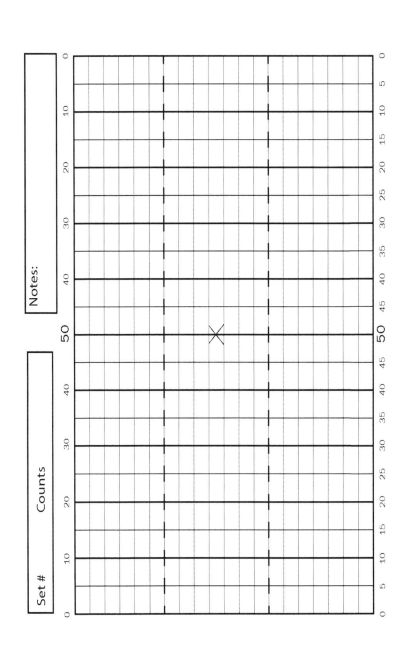

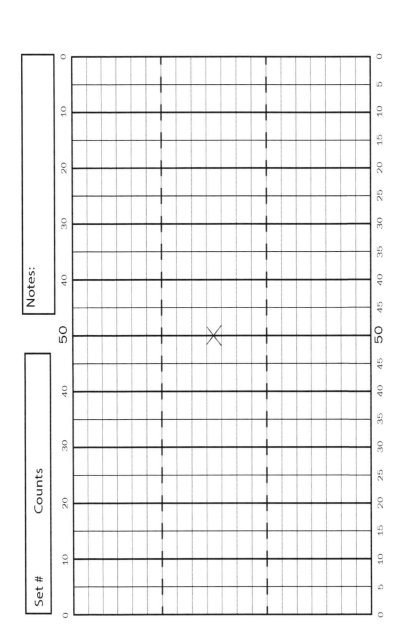

Notes:

Set #   Counts

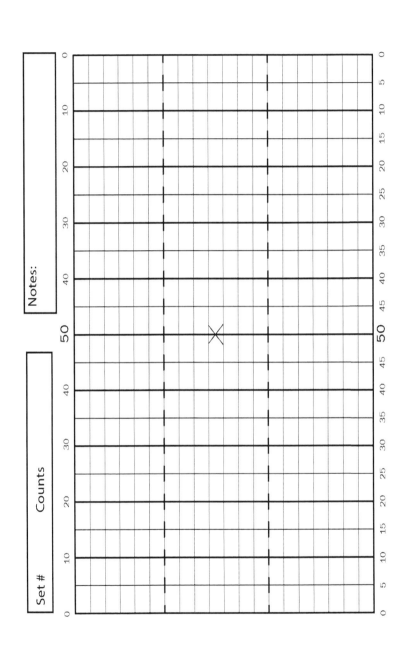

Notes:

Set #

Counts

Set #   Counts   Notes:

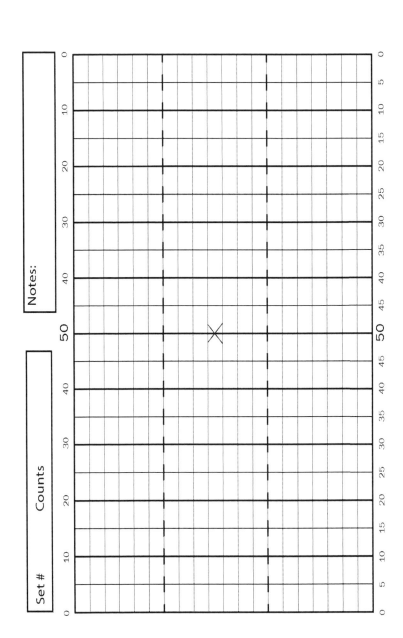

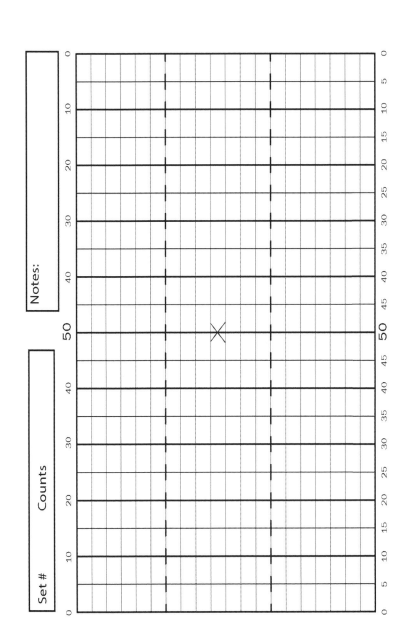

Set #   Counts

Notes:

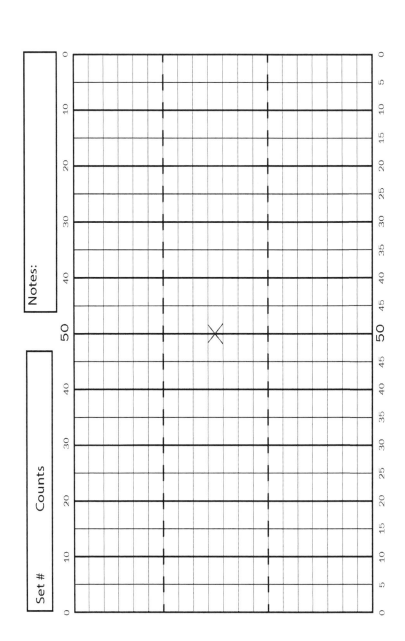

Set #   Counts

Notes:

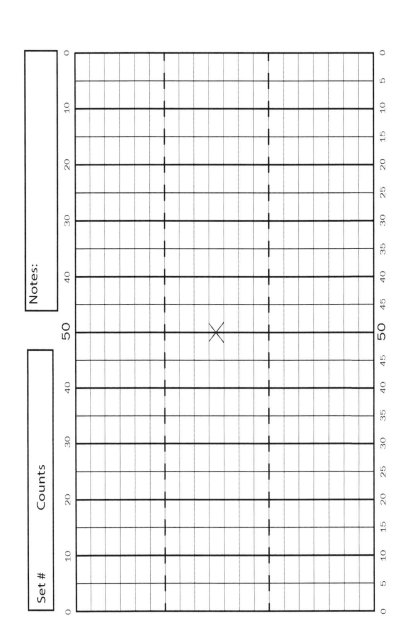

Set #   Counts

Notes:

Set #   Counts   Notes:

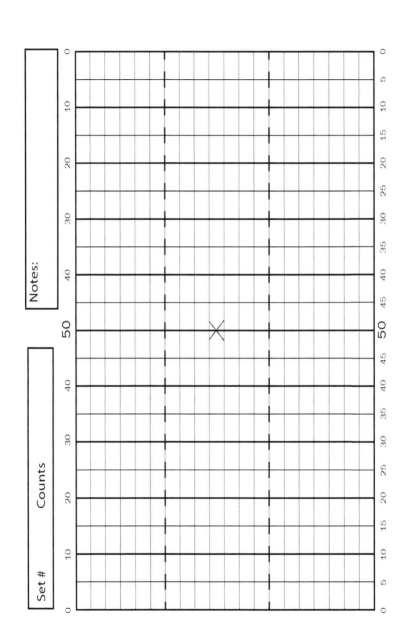

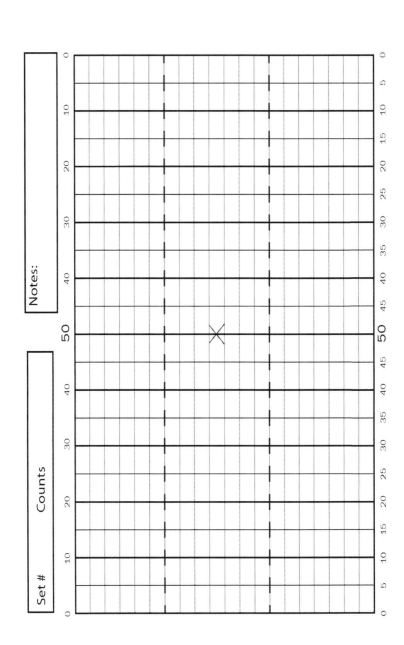

Set #　　Counts　　　Notes:

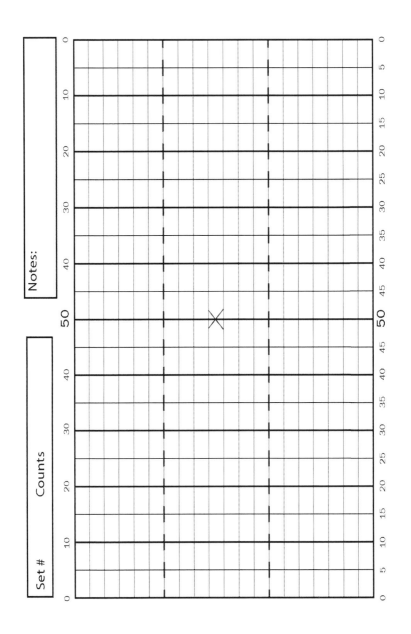

Notes:

Counts

Set #

Counts

Notes:

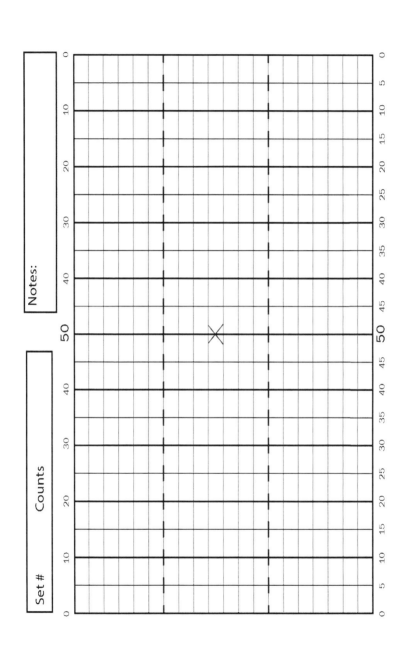

Set #   Counts   Notes:

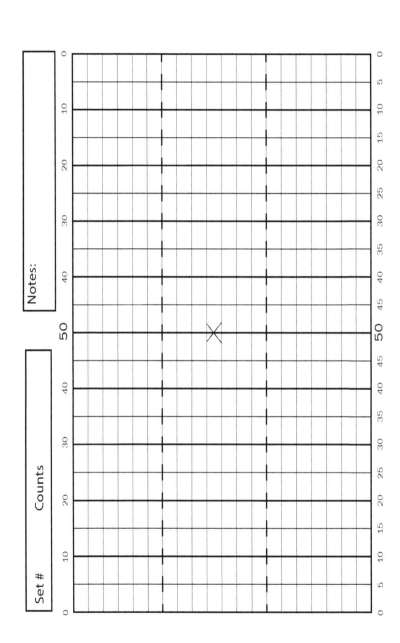

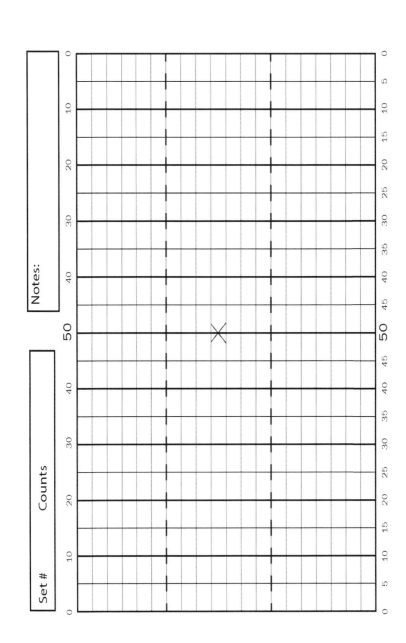

Set #   Counts   Notes:

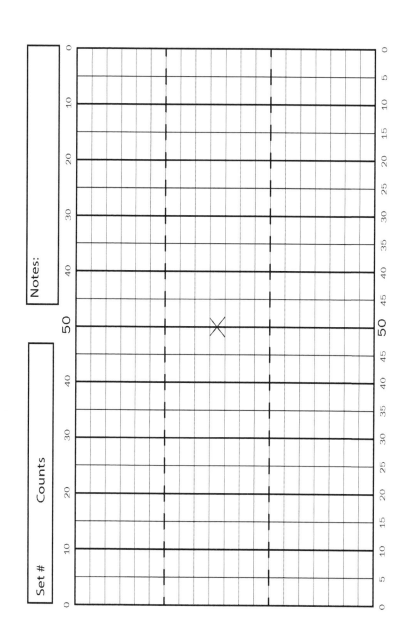

Notes:

Counts

Set #

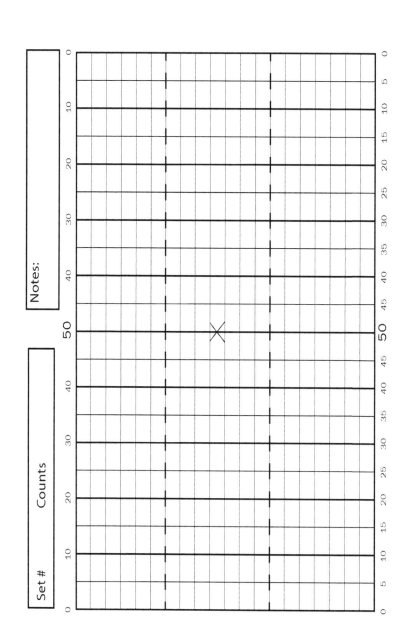

Set #

Notes:

Counts

Set #   Counts   Notes:

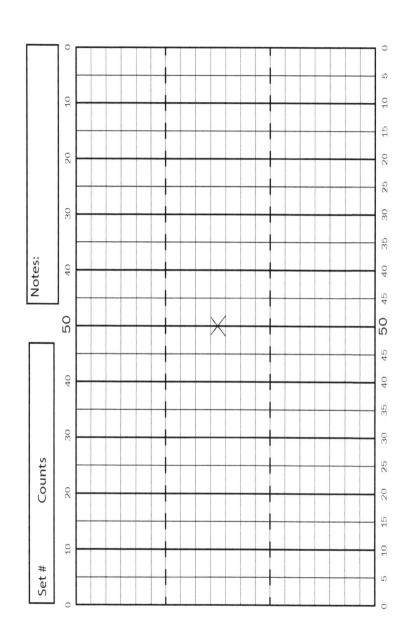

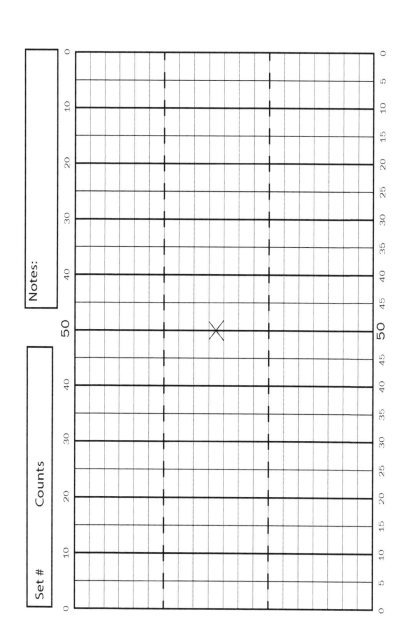

Set #   Counts   Notes:

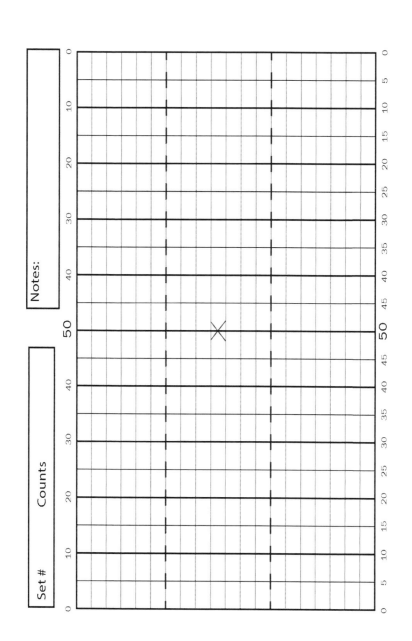

Notes:

Set #   Counts

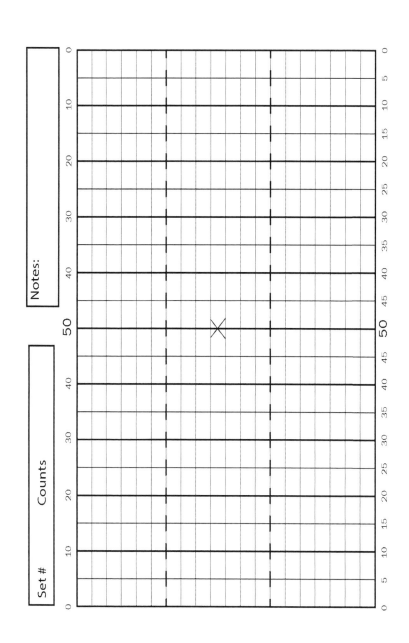

Notes:

Set #　　Counts

Notes:

Counts

Set #

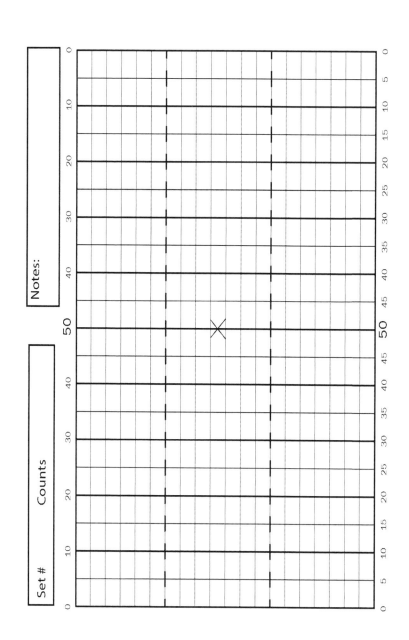

Notes:

Set #   Counts

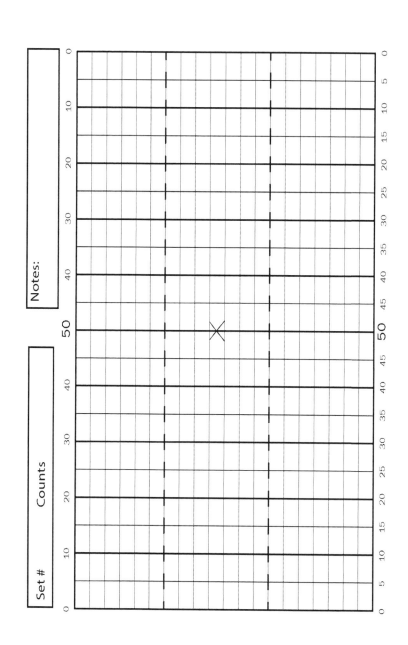

Set #   Counts

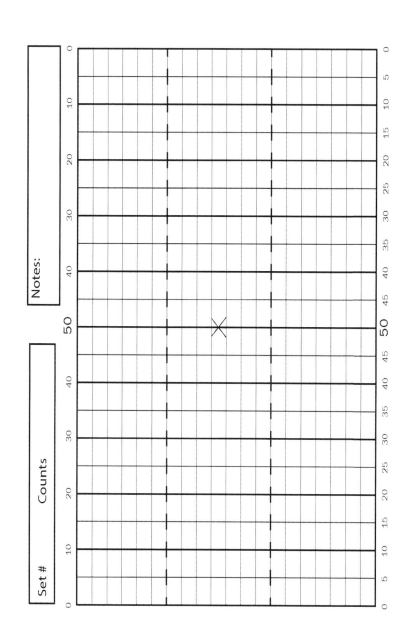

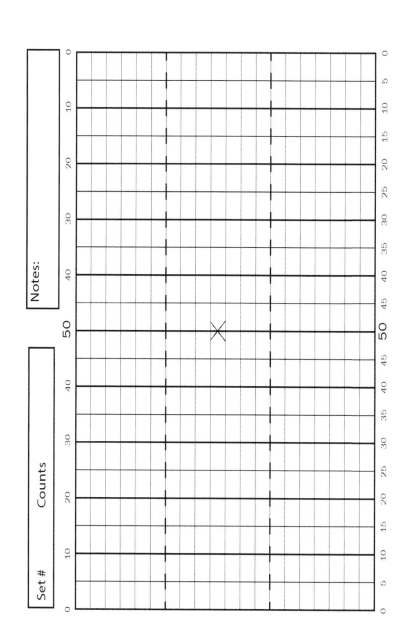

Notes:

Counts

Set #

Set #   Counts   Notes:

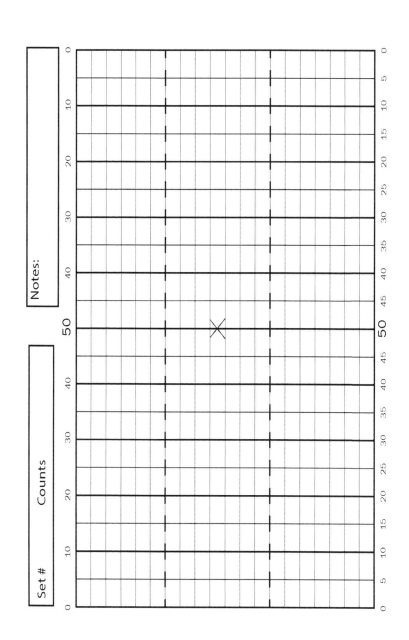

Set #   Counts

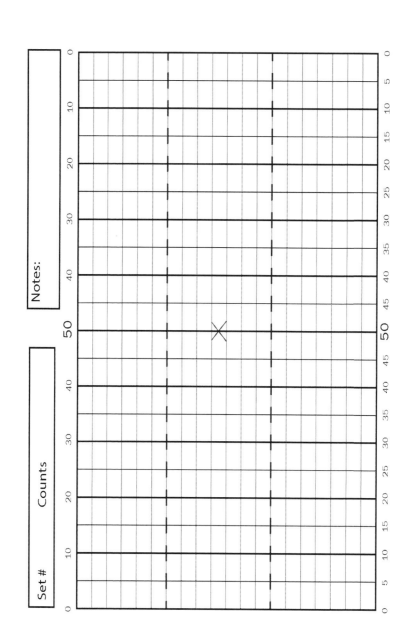

Set #   Counts

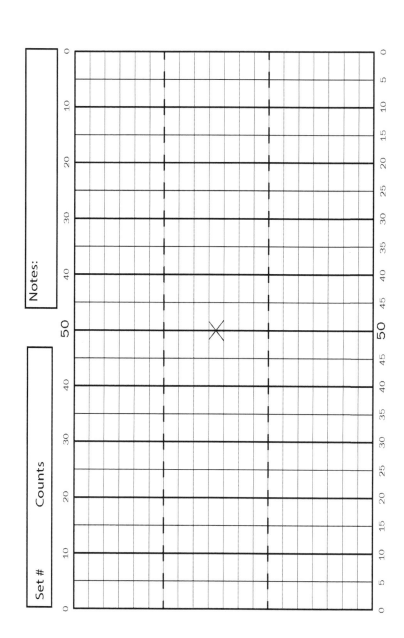

.

Set #   Counts   Notes:

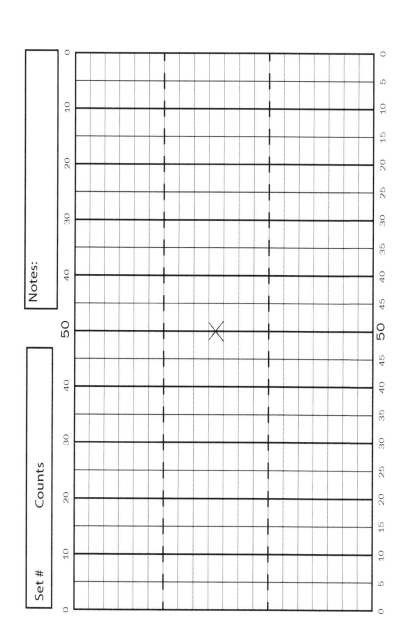

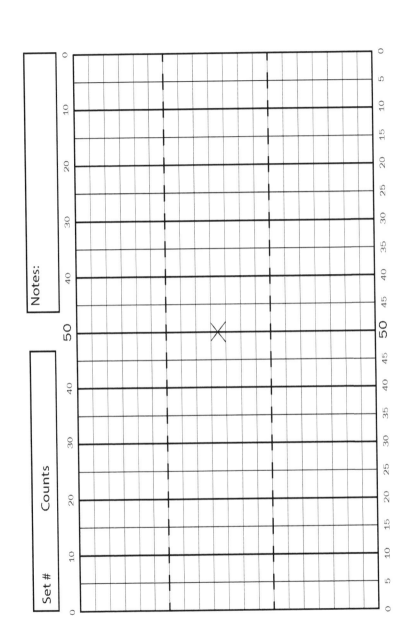

Set #   Counts   Notes:

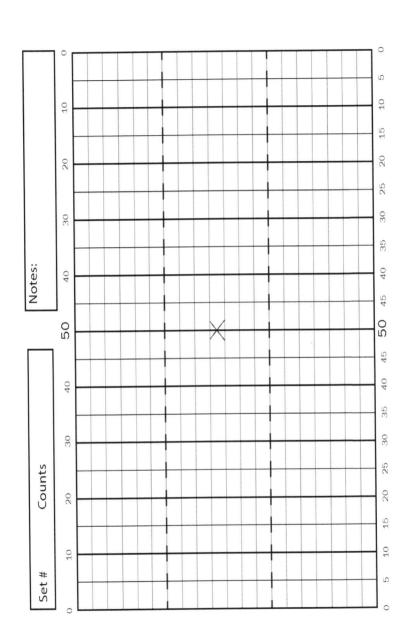

Made in the USA
San Bernardino, CA
21 July 2019